When Leaves Fall

by

Elise Skidmore

Heart Ally Books
Camano Island, Washington

Published by:
Heart Ally Books
26910 92nd Ave NW C5-406, Stanwood, WA 98292
Published on Camano Island, WA, USA
www.heartallybooks.com
ISBN-13: (epub) 978-0-9853740-4-4
ISBN-13: (paperback) 978-1-63107-005-1

Dedicated

To my family, past and present,
for their love and inspiration.
&
To Rosemary,
for always listening and being able
to make me laugh when I need it most.

Contents

When Leaves Fall	1
The River of Time	3
Today	4
Whaddaya Want?	5
Squirrel Dizain	6
Ever Your Child	7
You Gotta Believe	8
My Father Was Still A Boy	11
Seasonal Perspective	12
Blizzard	13
Lost In The Rain	14
Retirement Is Not An Option	15
Whenever I Hear	16
Object of Envy	17
Rejection	19
If You Loved Me	20
My Words	20
At the Zoo	21
Say Sorry	22
Friday the Thirteenth	23
Holiday Excess	25
More Than	27
Even Now	28
Not Fade Away	29
Something Shiny	30
Oak Tree	31
Living in the Shade	33
Unexpected	34
Surprise Pork Chops	35
Sunset Blush	37
Another Saturday Night	38
The Best Ever	39
Let's Dance	41
Treasure Chest	42
Sort of Strange	43
Desperation Shouts	44
Graveyard Shift	44
Insomnia	45
Doomsday	47
Monster Mash	48
Broken	49
The Night Visitor	50
Once Upon A Dream	51
Rest Assured	53
"Alice"	54
Sunrise at 10,000ft	55
Breaking Day	57
Of Poets and Poetry	58
Winter Crepuscule	59
The Trouble Is This	60
A Mistake Has Been Made	61
Blonde	62
Island Fantasy	63
I Am Not Addicted	64
Through a Microscope	66
100% Sure	67
Mix Up	68
Beautiful Words	69
Dear Norman	71
Stranger Kindness	72
Tsunami Haiku	73
Miracles happen	73
So Close	75
Also By Elise Skidmore	79

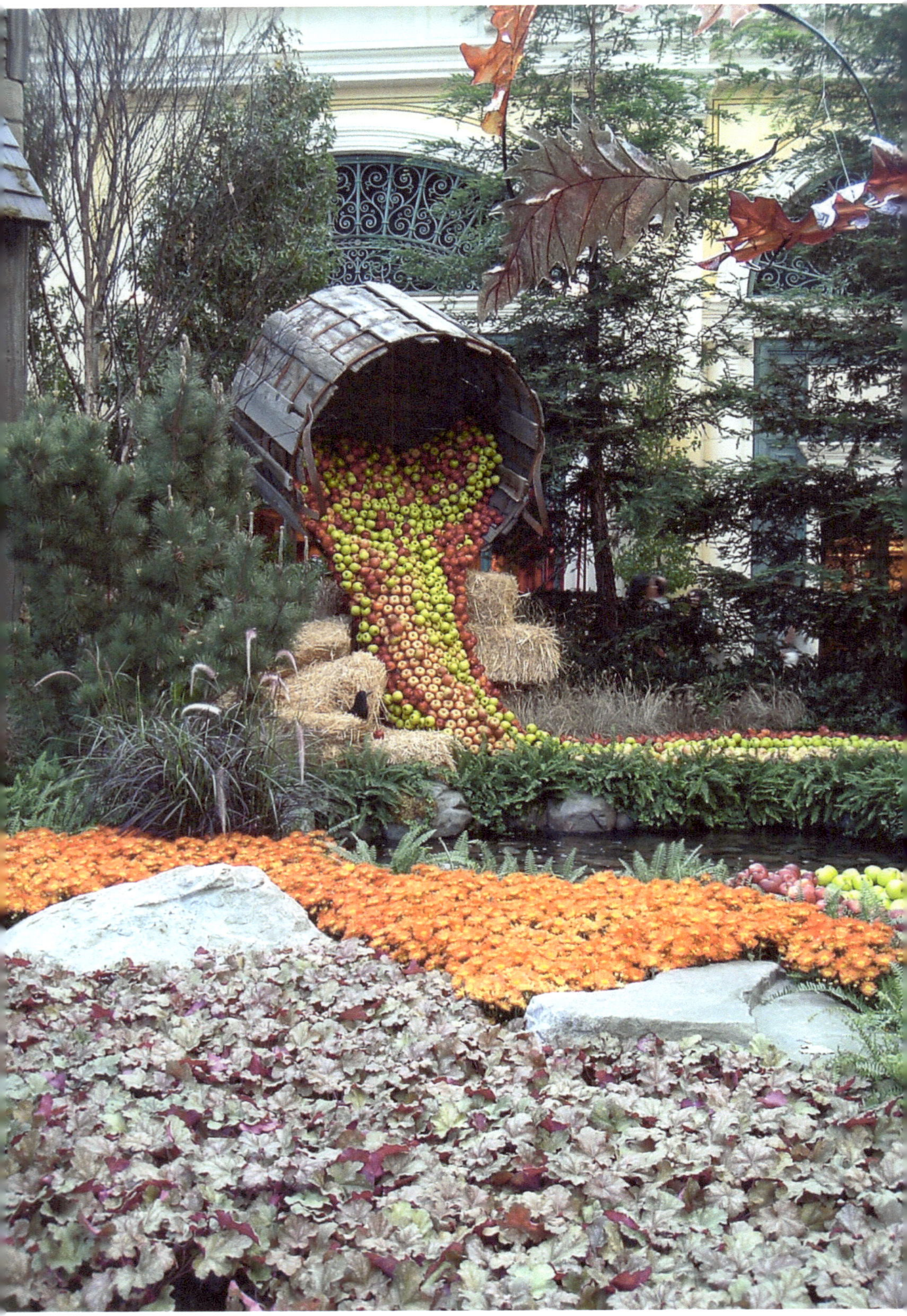

When Leaves Fall

When leaves fall,
still shouting life with
their last rasping breath,

as brilliant reds, yellows and umber
crunch beneath our feet,
I breathe deep,

inhaling sunshine, wood smoke
and memories of laughing
with the leaves
and you.

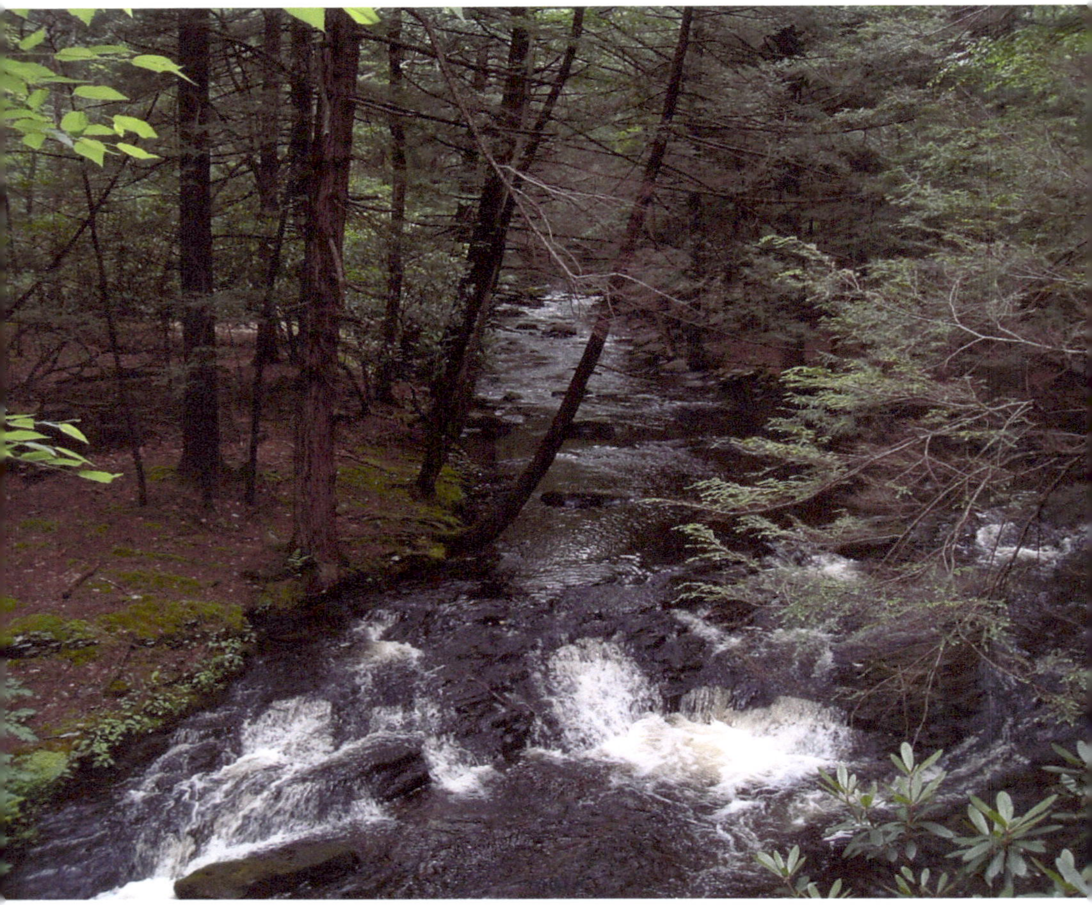

The River of Time

The river of time
exists all at once,
from its headwaters
to its estuaries.

We are trapped in its flow:
the people we once were
are the people we are now
and the people we will be.

We think we are different
but like the miracle of the Trinity
we are really only one
and cannot visit the perceived others,
who only exist in dreams.

No matter where we stand,
we are riding the rapids,
swirling in eddies,
meandering in the reaches
as the river goes on
forever.

Today

Most days I can outrun the melancholy,
focus on bright, happy memories
and let my spirit be lifted up.
But not today.

Today is your birthday.
It's sunny and mild,
a beautiful February day
with none of the snow
you always predicted.
I would be happy with snow
if it meant you were still here.

I wanted to get you a card
and struggle to find the perfect gift
to let you know
just how much I love you.
I wanted to pick up the phone
and hear your happiness
at the sound of my voice.
I wanted to knock on your door
and surprise you with a cake,
but I could do none of that.

Today I bought yellow roses.
Today, alone in a sea of cold white marble,
I sang Happy Birthday to you
and wished for the impossible
on invisible candles.

Whaddaya Want?

This is New York,
the Big Apple--
We got it all.
You could eat in a different place
every day for ten years
and never have the same thing twice--
and that's not even counting the street vendors.
Gotta love those dirty water hot dogs,
smothered in mustard and kraut,
and the smell of roasted chestnuts
when the shows let out.
You want fancy,
we got fancy,
but nothing beats
pastrami piled high on rye at the Carnegie Deli
or Lindy's New York Cheesecake.
So Whaddaya want?
We got it all.
But don't forget your wallet--
This is New York, after all.

Squirrel Dizain

A plump squirrel leaps along a bare branch,
his fur soft and warm against pale winter;
his anxious bounds create an avalanche
of new fallen snow come late to hinter-
land woods. Silent. There's nothing to splinter
the tranquil beat of Mother Nature's heart,
God's masterpiece, inspired work of art
that man savors and tries to imitate
with words, pictures, or music like Mozart;
all efforts fall short, no matter how great.

Ever Your Child

I am ever your child;
moving through the world
one day at a time,
step by slow step,
plodding slowly forward,
guided by the lessons you taught
and the examples you set,
always striving to be someone
worthy of your endless pride.

I am ever your child;
no matter how long you've been gone
there is a hole in my heart that aches
for your smile,
your voice,
your loving touch
that made all life's troubles
a little easier to bear.

I am ever your child.
You live within me
and still I am surrounded
by your boundless love.
But oh,
I miss you so.

You Gotta Believe

It was early baseball season
when I went to my first game
in May of 1969.
Mets vs. the Braves,
The Mets were the underdogs,
at the bottom of the league for seven years,
so even the great seats were cheap,
and boy, did we have great seats,
right down front along the first base line.
A bunch of school friends
enjoying the day and the game
until an obnoxious Braves' fan
with a fat cigar and a big mouth
began jeering our home team
with nasty personal remarks
we were sure the first baseman could hear.
We were just kids-- we didn't like it
but there was nothing we could do
to put an end to his poor sportsmanship.
But 1969 was a year for miracles,
and that sunny May afternoon was just the start.
The Mets' batters were hot and their runners fast,
with historic grand slams and runs per inning.

The score climbed higher;
our cheers grew louder--
the Braves' fan went silent.
Little did we know as we rode home
giddy with the joy of winning
that it wasn't just a fluke;
the Miracle Mets would win the World Series
and make believers of us all.
Forty-three years later
that day shines bright in memory
whenever the Mets play the Braves.
Once again I'm reminded that
miracles happen.

My Father Was Still A Boy

My father was still a boy
when he wrote stories
of a knight who came to life
in the Bremen town square
to save the world from itself.

My father was still a boy
when he stood up
for the things he believed in;
when he refused to salute a flag
that represented everything he despised,
and was beaten by an angry mob.

My father was still a boy
when he left his home,
his family, his friends.
Alone, at seventeen,
in a new country,
he built a better life
forged on courage and dreams of freedom.

My father was still a boy
if you measure by counting years,
but my father became a man
long before the battlefields of Europe
left their scars on his future dreams.

Seasonal Perspective

She thought it strange that two months ago,
the day's bright sunshine and sixty degree temperatures
would have warmed her with visions of early spring,
but today those sixty degrees left her chilled to the bone.
She wondered how that could be, as curled inside
her grandmother's afghan and sipping hot tea,
she wished for strong arms to enfold her.

Blizzard

The world
walled and weighted in white
buried in winter
beauty that leaves me cold
inside
hearts etched on frosted panes
crack in hoary glass

Lost In The Rain

You are lost to me like tears in the rain,
awash in the world that surrounds me.
I know you are out there, somewhere,
that you think of me as I think of you.
I know that love survives;
like energy that cannot die,
it simply changes forms.
I know you didn't leave by choice.
Even armed with that knowledge
I am not satisfied.
I want what I cannot have--
your embrace when I'm feeling blue,
your smile when I enter a room.
I cannot bring you back,
not with wishes or more tears,
so I stand in the rain
and pretend it's your kiss.

Retirement Is Not An Option

Winter is not a season; it's an occupation.
--Sinclair Lewis

Vacations are possible,
but we cannot escape winter
nor its frigid beauty.
Whether the weather
or the season of our lives,
winter always comes
with shovels.
If we are lucky
we can look back on
diamonds glittering in the sun
and a job well done.

Whenever I Hear

Whenever I hear
Glen Miller's "In The Mood"
I think of you--

how you'd smile and say,
"That's from my era!"

how you'd tap your foot
and snap your fingers
in that funny way that
never made a sound

how it was the one song
that got you on the dance floor
even though you had two left feet

Whenever I hear
Glen Miller's "In The Mood"
I think of you
and my heart smiles.

Object of Envy

Oh, lucky begonia
wilting in the clay pot--
someone noticed
your sad state!

With light and love,
they will nurture you
back to full vigor,
and your pretty pink smile
will brighten the world once again.

Rejection

Filled with anger,
churning with stress,
slowly turning him
into another person,
I wanted to help--
to ease his pain somehow,
to bring laughter back to his heart.
I tried everything I knew,
but it came back to me
in piercing shards
smashed against
a wall of negativity.
With nothing left to do,
I gather up the pieces
and wait.

If You Loved Me

Don't start the
If You Loved Me game.
Like Tic-Tac-Toe,
there's no way to win
and I refuse to play.
I won't barter with love;
even though I have plenty in reserve,
it's too precious to risk losing
over such silliness.
You know I love you.
I wouldn't be here if I didn't.

Here is the only place
I want to be.

My Words

My lips are moving
but you don't hear
my words
linger in dead space
stopped cold by your body language
Actions speak louder than words
They shout your intent
The windows to your soul
have the shades pulled tight
The lights are on
but nobody's home
to listen
to my words

At the Zoo

Mountain gorilla
stares thoughtfully through the glass
his soul in his eyes
His mate and children cuddle
as if no one is watching

Say Sorry

Whoever said
love means never having to say you're sorry
didn't get it quite right.
Sometimes love means having to say you're sorry
even when you're not,
because you know the other person
never will.
They won't—or can't,
not because they aren't sorry--
usually they are,
they just aren't capable of saying the words,
whether from a childhood trauma
or a deep-seeded personality trait.
Whatever the reason,
sometimes you have to let them off the hook,
because you love them.
The other side of the coin
is loving them enough
to hear the unspoken apologies.

Friday the Thirteenth

You had a superstiticus streak;
you thought Friday the thirteenth unlucky
because that was the day
the doctors screwed up and you died
on the operating table.
It was the day you saw your long dead family
and the beautiful bright light;
It was the day you floated above yourself
and watched the doctors working.
You swore Friday the thirteenth was unlucky.

I argued to the contrary.
How could it be unlucky
when the doctors brought you back to life?
You had to admit that was a good point.

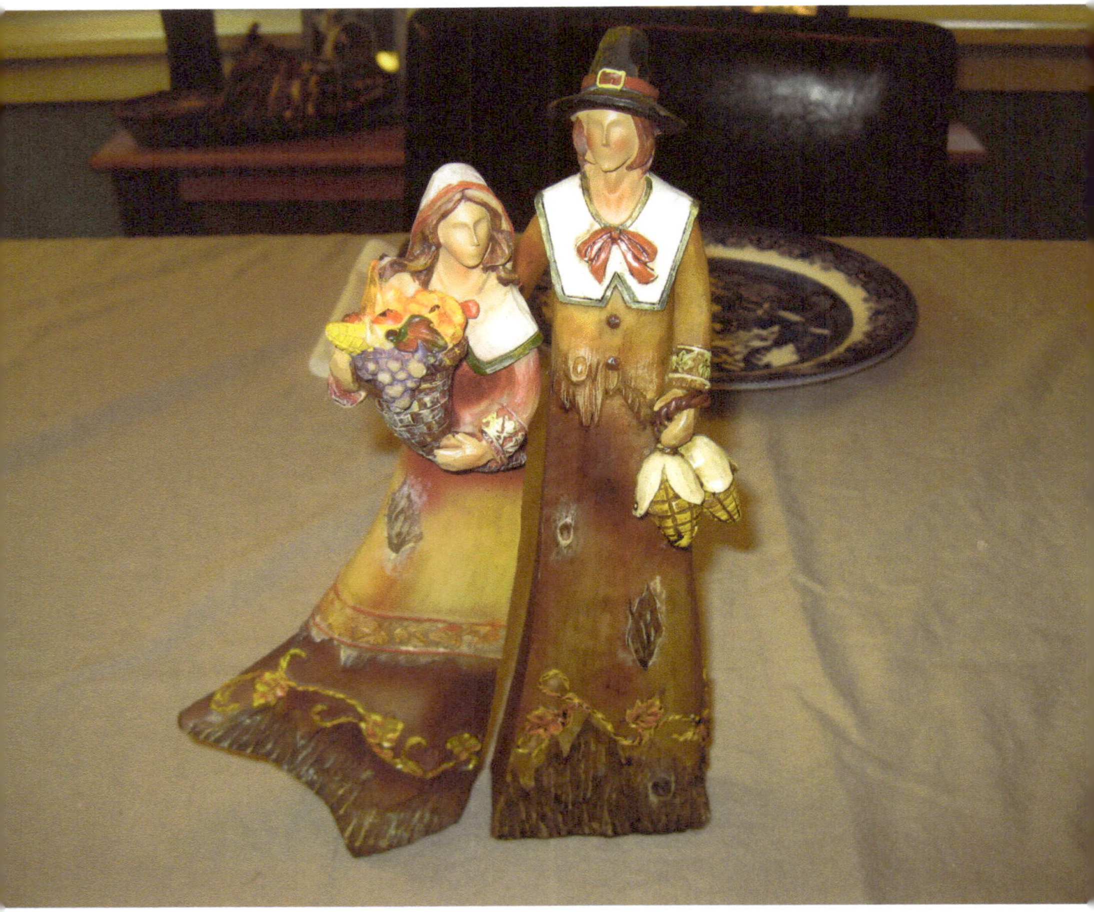

Holiday Excess

Excess often has a negative connotation,
especially when linked to the holidays.
Too much work,
too much food,
too much waste,
too much commercialism and money spent--
it cannot be denied.
Yet when I think about holidays past,
those excesses have a very small part.

I remember watching the Macy's parade
Thanksgiving morning
and tearing loaves of bread into little pieces
for my mother's stuffing;
the house was filled
with the smell of roasting turkey
that we only got to eat once a year.
In our small apartment,
the furniture was pushed aside
and the french doors opened
between the bedroom and living room
to accommodate the extended family
who came to share the feast.
Yes, there was always too much food,
but it never went to waste;
we dined on leftovers for days
and loved it.

All the little traditions,
the happiness of being together,
laughter shared with loved ones--
those are the things I remember most.
Sometimes excess is a very good thing.

More Than

How much do I love you?

More than
the feathers exploding from a down pillow
or dandelion fluff adrift on a spring day

More than
the champagne bubbles fizzing in my glass
or the number of text messages sent in a day

I love you more
than Mozart wrote notes
or Faulkner wrote words

It doesn't matter
if you're cross or not your best self
I love you
more than
enough to hold true
until the worst is past
and once again
you are the one
I love
more

Even Now

I can see Mama's black marble composition notebook
with its lined pages
opened to reveal hand-copied quotations
and poems she fancied.
I can still hear her read bits of Ogden Nash aloud:
his purple cow and its sequel.
There are newspaper clippings
held with cellophane tape that yellowed with time,
along with pamphlet programs
from concerts in the park,
where we sat in the grass sharing
pitchers of beer and lemonade
from the refreshment stand
while the band played on.
When we grew bored with the music
my sister and I were soothed with promises
of a ride on the carousel when it was done.
What fun, on a warm summer evening,
to ride around and around
with the strung lights dancing as we passed by.
Even now,
when Mama's makeshift scrapbook
is long gone to who knows what end,
I remember the little things
she thought were important.
My heart is filled with volumes of them.

Not Fade Away

It's been such a long time,
but you've never really gone.
You linger along the fringes of my heart,
waiting for some random thing
to pull you into the spotlight.

Like the end of an old record
where the song never ends,
only repeats and repeats
until the refrain fades away,
leaving its echo dancing in my brain.

Something Shiny

At the edge of my peripheral vision,
something shiny winked at me
from the dark corner of the basement
where no one had ventured for decades.
Upon investigation I found
a brand new dime of polished silver,
and I knew you were there.

Oak Tree

You were the oak tree
always standing tall and strong
for your family
the acorns that you planted
live and thrive in your memory

Living in the Shade

She liked sunny days,
but wasn't a sun-worshiper.
She always walked
on the shady side of the street.
At family picnics she made a point
of sitting where the umbrella
would protect her from the sun.

There was the time at the zoo,
when we had to search for a table under the trees
before we could stop for lunch.
She waited patiently,
enjoying the dappled light through the leaves
and warm air on her skin,
listening to her grandchildren chattering like little monkeys
while the others went to the concession stand.

A sudden splat from a bird in the branches
landed on her forehead;
the children erupted in a chorus
of mingled groans and giggles.
She pulled a tissue from her pocket
and wiped the mess away.
Smiling, she said,
"It's good luck."

Unexpected

(for Sarah)

It's time you spread your wings
and fly from the nest.
From the moment you arrived
I knew someday you would go,
for that is the way of things--
what is meant to be.
To realize you are capable and smart,
that you will succeed in life
is a parent's fondest wish come true,
and I rejoice for your happiness.

You haven't gone far
and we have almost as much contact
as when you were here,
what with four jobs and a social life
that kept you running in and out;
and there are still pieces of you
everywhere I turn
as if you hadn't gone at all.

The strange emptiness I felt
when I left you at your new house,
and the lump in my throat
as I drove home
without you
was unexpected.

Surprise Pork Chops

It's been an exhausting week.
What with one thing and another,
cooking meals wasn't really on the menu.
Take out, sandwiches, and frozen foods won the day--
or should I say week?
Imagine my surprise this afternoon
when I opened the meat drawer
and found the wrapped up pork chops
I bought when shopping last Sunday.
They didn't look bad—smelled okay too.
I was raised not to waste food or money
(Remember the starving children in China!
Do you think money grows on trees?!)
What to do?
Should I take a chance that some terrible bacteria
hadn't left its spawn just waiting to make me sick?
In the end I decided to push my luck
and tempt the fates.
Seasoned and baked to perfection,
they tasted pretty good,
if I do say so myself.
Best of all,
I'm still alive to tell the tale.

Sunset Blush

Sunset blushing pink
like rose petals on water
reminds me of you
the white foam laps at the shore
your hand's soft touch on my cheek

Another Saturday Night

He sits on the sofa
with his legs propped up on the coffee table.
He doesn't care that the TV is blasting
a rerun of a movie he's seen a hundred times.
All he wants is to be free of the world for a while,
to let his mind and body go limp
and just relax.

She sits beside him on the sofa,
not at all interested in the beaches of Normandy
blowing up on the screen in front of her.
He stretches a leg across her lap
and she massages his aching knee,
until her arm grows tired.

He takes her hand in his,
their fingers entwine.
From the corner of her eye
she sees his eyelids droop.
It isn't long before soft snores fill the room
and she reaches for the remote.

The Best Ever

Your smile
the first time we met
crinkled your cheeks
and danced in your eyes.
Your smile
when our eyes met
across a crowded airport terminal
made me giddy with joy,
like champagne bubbles
dancing in my heart.
Your smile
says, "I love you,"
without making a sound.
Your smile
is the best gift
you ever gave me.

Let's Dance

They're playing our song,
the one that said all the things
we felt but were too shy to say out loud.
Take me in your arms
the way you did back then,
when love was new
and the world filled with promise.
Hold me so close,
I can feel your heart beating
as you softly sing in my ear.
There's only you and me--
Let's dance.

Treasure Chest

An autographed photo
signed with bold, black slashes,
a Phantom mask with its strap broken,
and a flattened birthday balloon--
treasured memories kept safe
in a leather chest at the foot of the bed.
The gem in her collection,
her most prized possession,
the button from his coat
that came free in her hand
when he kissed her
that first goodnight.

Sort of Strange

It's sort of strange,
like we've gone back to the beginning,
but encased in the remnants of time passed.
It's the same house with much of the same furnishings
as it had three decades ago,
though we are all showing our age these days.
The photographs tell the story.
We were two, then three, then four,
and the house breathed
with love and laughter--
and some tears too.
Now we are two again,
holding hands as we share
the love seat in front of the TV,
just as we've always done.
We exchange our days between commercials
and I watch your eyelids droop,
weighted and weary from too many long hours;
you fight to stay awake,
but I listen to your soft snore and know
exhaustion has won another round.
With gentle fingers I stroke your hair,
thinking of the things I must do before it's time
for us to climb the stairs to the bed
where we repeat our nighttime mantra,
still true after so many years.
The lights are out.
The house is silent.
Only the two of us now.
Side by side,
as we've always been,
we sleep and dream
together.

Desperation Shouts

Desperation shouts
drowning out the joy in life
Hope still whispers from
the deep corners of the heart
Listen to its voice

Graveyard Shift

Driving home from work
when the graveyard shift is done
he longs for his bed
unaware the world would change
when the car ran the red light

Insomnia

When night nestles sleep on every head but mine,
I toss and turn and pace trails in the carpet,
wondering why I am resistant to its somnolent potions
while others easily drift away on a sea of dreams.

Wishing my thoughts would still,
that the voice chiding my brain, scolding,
"Sleep. Sleep. Morning comes early,"
would just shut up and let me rest,
I wrestle with the night.

The sound of the wind gently rattling the windows
mingles with the snores of loved ones lost in the Land of Nod;
Worn out and weary, I stare at the ceiling and listen
to the heat clink and clang along the baseboards.

I pray for sleep that will not come.
Not with late night movies or leaden tomes.
When all is lost, and I cry defeat,
I let the words flow from withered brain to page.

Finally, drained and spent, I sleep,
knowing exhaustion will shadow me when the sun rises.

Doomsday

They say the end is near.
Some days I think it can't come soon enough,
especially when faced with bleak visions
of a post apocalyptic future
where mankind loses all pretense of the "kind".
Utopias are scarce on the ground
and even those in fiction never seem to end well.

I try not to think about it much.
It's not as if I can do anything to stop it.
With luck I'll have left this earthly coil long before,
or barring that be at ground zero when it happens.
Whether the end comes
from Man or God's folly,
I'm sure the aftermath won't be pretty.

Monster Mash

Frankenstein wasn't a bad fellow,
just created from bits and pieces,
mostly just confused and misunderstood.

Are Dracula and his brethren
so different from the bloodsuckers of big business,
mesmerizing their prey to get what they crave?
At least in the vampires' case,
it's a matter of life and death,
not just accrued wealth.

It might be argued that women
and werewolves have much in common,
turning into wild beasts with the cycles of the moon--
though werewolves in fiction are
almost always portrayed as male.

Ghosts and goblins,
demons and other things
that go bump in the night
may be creations of human imagination,
meant to entertain or
help us face our fears,
But beware--
Monsters live inside us all.

Broken

Awakened from sleep
by calls from a frightened child
I stumbled in the darkness;
reaching for a light,
I found a flight of stairs instead.
I lay at the bottom
scraped and bruised,
with wrists turned at odd angles,
both broken as it turned out.

At the hospital
they had to cut off the wedding ring
that had been there
since the moment my husband
slipped it on my finger
so many years before.
I cried then at the pain,
worse than the two broken wrists.

A silly thing, I know.
Our bond was not broken
with the severed ring;
it was, in fact, made stronger.
There is a notch visible in the design,
left from the repair.
It is small
and I am the only one
who realizes it's there.
Still, it hurts my heart to see it.

The Night Visitor

She lingers beside the bed
where her child sleeps,
just as she always did before;
invisible in the deep night,
unseen even by the fat ginger cat
curled tight on the rug.

She strokes blond curls
with gentle fingers,
while she watches the
rhythmic rise and fall
of her child's breathing.
Her child, once so small,
she carried her under her heart,
now grown, but still
and always her baby.

She leaves a feathered kiss on her baby's brow,
filled with a lifetime of mother's love.
When the sweet smile spreads
across the sleeping lips,
she knows she can
rest in peace.

Once Upon A Dream

Once upon a dream
the sun was shining;
you were standing here
with arms open wide,
waiting for me
to step into your embrace.

Though I knew it was a dream,
and told you so,
you simply smiled.
Without a word
you bid me come,
and so I did.

You hugged me so tight,
the way you always did.
I felt it to my core.
When I awoke
there were tears in my eyes;
your touch was still warm on my skin,
and I knew
you were with me.

Rest Assured

She woke in the dark
to the touch of his hand in her hair,
his fingers a gentle caress,
as if to reassure himself
that she was still there,
alive and breathing beside him,
and wondered at the unexpected tenderness.
In sleepy contentment
she patted his hip
to let him know
she was right where she should be,
then settled back
into sweet dreams.

"Alice"

At first, I thought it was bad luck to fall
down the rabbit's hole; in a way it was
lucky too. I merely ended in a sprawl
without damage 'cept to my pride which was

lucky indeed, since I had to give chase.
How could I not pursue such a bunny,
dressed as he was in ruffles and fine lace?
His associates, too, were quite funny:

talking caterpillars and grinning cats,
hatters, dormice, and an army of cards.
The Queen of Hearts' repeating caveat,
"Off With Her Head" I could not disregard.

But lessons I've learned from my bizarre dream,
nothing's impossible or too extreme.

Sunrise at 10,000ft

High on Haleakala's peak
we stand in cold pre-dawn darkness,
awed by heaven's dome of diamonds above us.
If half the wishes sent on these shooting stars come true,
We and all we love will never want for anything.
A single seam of light stretches on the horizon.
Standing close in anxious anticipation,
like children waiting to glimpse Santa Claus,
we watch for the sun to rise above the clouds.
When it does, time stops to listen
to the universe's orchestra
playing a silent symphony inside our soul;
and like the new day,
we are filled with light and born anew.

Breaking Day

The rising sun gleams through the window;
it waits for no one.
It cares not for the whims of man,
whether he has worked hard--
or played harder,
or has the day off
to spend as he wants.
Even when storm clouds
block its brilliance,
the sun always rises
on its own schedule
and takes its rest when it chooses.
Sometimes I wonder
if the sun ever feels like sleeping in,
but some greater power
that will not wait
forces him to break the day.

Of Poets and Poetry

It is
simplicity
the speaking with silence
between the words that give meaning
to life

Three cheers
Poetry thrives
and will continue on
as long as beautiful dreamers
awake

to view
the universe
as it is and might be
caught in shadows encased in light
It lives

and breathes
in poets' hearts
enlightened souls made rich
with fecund imagination's
insight

Winter Crepuscule

Silhouetted in morning moonlight
bare branches sway in the wind;
a line of giants, whispering;
trees telling winter secrets
to squirrels and birds who find sanctuary
even in their naked limbs.

I am so cold.
I listen to the susurrous soughing
of the trees as they lean to and fro,
wondering if they know
when spring will come again.

The Trouble Is This

The trouble is this--
I know that I should,
but I don't want to,
and deep down I know
that if I really don't want to,
I won't.
It isn't smart or logical,
but it's the truth.
I also think it's part of being human.

Everyone knows
smoking, drugs,
excessive drinking,
over-eating
and all that jazz
are bad for you,
and will likely shorten your life span.
But no one stops
until they've reached their breaking point;
the place where they know deep inside
they want to make the change
because the pain and anguish
of not changing is greater than
staying the same.

So that's the trouble.
The real problem is
how do I stop being human?

A Mistake Has Been Made

A mistake has been made.
Whoever is in charge
of the grand scheme of things
screwed up royally.
My dream house was meant to be
perpetually clean--
i.e., self-cleaning.

I was meant for better things
than cleaning toilets,
dusting, vacuuming,
washing dishes and scrubbing floors.
I keep putting it off,
expecting someone else
to take care of it,
(the Brownies, maybe?)
but they never do.

Something is very wrong here.
The housework is not taking care of itself.
The clutter grows deeper and
if it's true what they say about dust
being largely composed of human skin,
there's enough of it here that
I should be able to create
a butler,
a couple of maids,
and a hunky lawn boy
to take care of things.

Maybe I should make some time
to research the possibilities
tomorrow.

Blonde

Let me speak very slowly
so you won't have any trouble understanding,
and I'll try not to use words
you'll need to look up in the dictionary.

I'm not stupid
and I've never been promiscuous
or needed a brain transplant
in order to change a light bulb,
or confused a Porsche with a porch.

In fact, I graduated with honors --
and I didn't have to dye my hair to do it.

I have to wonder,
if blondes are so dumb,
then why does everyone want to be one?
Seems to me all the famous bombshells
were blonde wannabes --
does that make them stupid
or just jealous?

If you want my opinion
-- and maybe you don't
'cause I'm just a 'dumb blonde' --
I think the ditziness is just one side effect
of too much bleach seeping through to the brain.

Island Fantasy

White sand beach
below brilliant blue skies,
surrounded by bluer water,
dusted with diamonds
in the sun.
Palm trees slow dance
with the gentle breeze
that brings sweet hibiscus
wafting on the air,
while sea birds play.
Two chairs,
side by side,
an icy pitcher of margaritas,
and you.
Perfection.

I Am Not Addicted

I am not addicted,
though some might think differently,
countering with shouts of "Denial!"
That's not the case at all.
I am fully aware
of the time spent sitting at the computer,
reading email,
paying bills,
shopping,
sorting digital photos,
browsing the internet,
managing websites,
playing games at FaceCrack,
and even writing.

Were I truly addicted
I'd have a smart phone that would keep me
connected 24/7,
no matter where I am
or who I am with;
I'd have a laptop
for the same purpose
and wouldn't leave home
without one or the other.

As it is, I have neither.
I can go out to dinner,
socialize with friends,
and even go on vacation
without a thought to
what I might be missing.

I repeat—I am not addicted.
Though I admit that
playing catch-up is a bitch.

Through a Microscope

Through a microscope
even miniscule is big
Unseen life abounds
In the universe we are
an unseen dot on a slide

100% Sure

I know I packed all the chargers,
the medications and toiletries,
the one extra outfit for "just in case".
I know I put a hold on the paper
and a friend is taking care of the mail.
The cell phone is fully charged
and there's plenty to read on my Kindle.
I double-checked all the locks,
and made certain all appliances were turned off.
My keys, my wallet and passport
are tucked in my bag,
cash and credit cards good to go.
I'm 100% sure I haven't forgotten anything.
So why do I have this niggling feeling
that I have?

Mix Up

Roast beef on rye bread
with lettuce and mayonnaise
I am craving lunch
Open PBJ on white
Damn! I grabbed the wrong bag

Beautiful Words

She wasn't glamorous like showgirls or celebrities,
and even though she met few of society's requirements
she believed she was beautiful.
She saw her beauty in the faces of her children,
whose smiles inspired awe and could bring tears to her eyes,
and knew their beauty was part of her.

Still she wished to hear the words, freely given,
whispered in her ear,
and read their truth in his eyes.

Dear Norman

Solid citizens
living everyday
in a Rockwell painting

They smile
visiting the kindly ol' doc
or consoling a friend
going fishing
or off to war

Even when things are bad
life's never dismal
and hope glimmers in every eye
The canvas may be flat
but life is 3-dimensional

I'd like to pull back the paint
and step into their world
walk down the street
dragging a stick along the white picket fence
whistling a tune
while a playful puppy-partner
laps at my heels
and the worst punishment I can expect
is Old Lady Smith's frowning countenance

Stranger Kindness

Had she thought about what she was doing,
she never would have done it,
but seeing the desolation
on his wide-eyed moppet's face
as he sat on the curb
watching the traffic zip by him,
with his chin resting on his open palms,
as if he carried the weight of the world
inside his head,
she couldn't have done anything
but what she did.

Her knees cracked when
she sat down beside him,
but no one heard
amid the bustle of the city.
When she draped a comforting arm
over his shoulder,
he stiffened
and turned to see who dared
invade his empty space.
She did the only thing she could--
she gave him her smile,
filled with sunshine and hope,
and watched the light
dawn in his eyes.

Tsunami Haiku

The cherry blossoms
still bloom after tsunamis
Somehow I will too

Miracles happen

Miracles happen
with every inhalation
with every heart beat
Open your eyes wide and see
rainbows inside the bubble

So Close

So close
just a quiet thought away
that's where you are

now and forever

sweet sustenance
to nourish and succor

alone and hard pressed
I wish you were here
and then you are

so close
just a quiet thought away

touchstone for the rest

pitiable lot
who always fall short
of being you

With eyes closed
and heart open
you are so close

just a quiet thought away

Acknowledgements

I would like to thank Lisa Norman, my friend and publisher, for all of her hard work and patience. Without her, having two books published would still be a wish saved for starry nights.

I would also like to thank my fellow writers at SectionSixx and TCU for their support, encouragement, and generally nudging me to write more.

And a very special thank you to Diana Gabaldon, whose wonderful books led me to a community of writers at Compuserve that changed my life forever. Her talent has been an inspiration; her friendship, encouragement, and generosity, an invaluable gift.

Also By Elise Skidmore

Poems from the Edge of Spring

A book of poetry from Elise Skidmore touching on the phases and
loves of life, family, friends and the world we find ourselves in.
Elise is converting poetry haters into poetry lovers with her ac-
cessible poems that delight and entertain.

Look for *Poems from the Edge of Spring* at Amazon, Barnes & Noble,
iTunes, and wherever paperback or ebooks are sold.

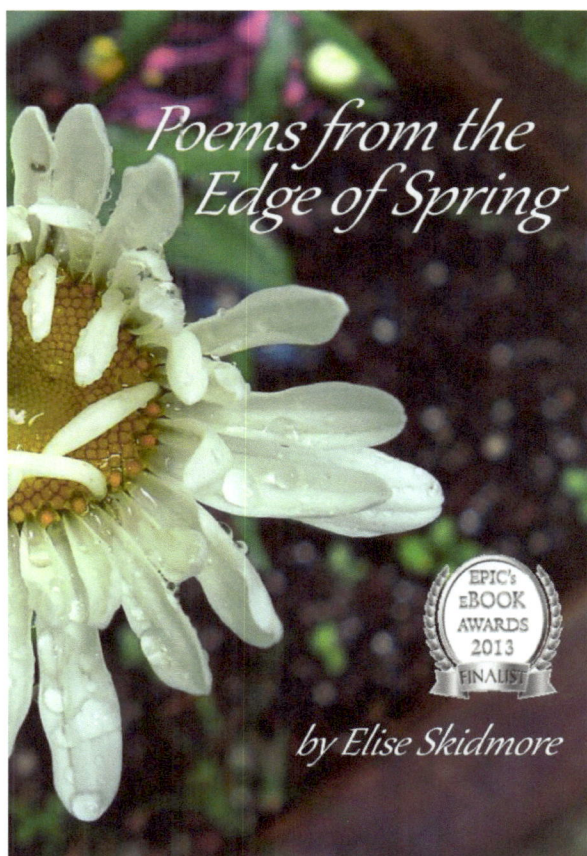

You can also find a digital copy of *When Leaves Fall* wherever
ebooks are sold.

www.ingramcontent.com/pod-product-compliance
Lightning Source LLC
Chambersburg PA
CBHW042128080426
42735CB00001B/11